MW01230626

HIGHLY FAVORED

By: Lauren Sanaa B.D.

INTRO:

2019 has been one of the most weird, emotional (as in different emotions literally), unnecessarily stressful years of my life. But a very educational, eye opening, and revealing one too.

-Lauren Sanaa B.D.

Table of Contents

R.A.P:

Saved me from me.

Add Bars Here:

_____

_____

_____

_____

_____

_____

_____

_____

2019:

These days
Seem to be getting shorter
And shorter
I lay down
Expecting a message
From a dream
An explanation
I prayed
For the wrong thing
Knowing that whatever came
Would be temporary
I ignored
The fact that I
Should make positive
Direct
Affirmations
Which caused my blessings
To vary

Time
Must
Not be on my side
Negativity won't leave me

And positivity won't stay long enough
To let me make something of it
But honestly who am I
To complain
When I can turn on a light
To write and speak
On my luck
When can I turn on my shower
And know that 9 times out of 10
The water
Won't kill me
Or when can I look in my circle
And see no snakes or empty space
Am I just unaware
Of what can't I see
What do I not need
To appreciate

Pen Game

Pick up a pen turn some heads.
Pick up a pen and change your life.
Pick up a pen and sign a deal.
Pick up a pen and $pin the wheel.
Pick up a pen but watch what you say.
We take what you say very serious
nowadays.

- The youth

.

Cylindrical
Forces

I've been running ever since sunsets
Stopped selling seeds to my chakras.
They call it lyrical healing.

I'm numb to the feeling of needles
Scratching at my tapes.
Stumbly subscriptions silence

My subtle sentential salvations

Of thought and reason

Before consciousness does.

Shook the hood

off my shoulders and set it

on my

heart.

Self-consciousness

And selfish type determination.

If I was Rich

If I was rich I would send
Every Detroit Public School
Student to Africa
For 1 month
And tell them to come back with ideas
On building
A Wakanda
In their community.

What's Over There in the Tall Grass?

Ain't no garbage over there,

Ain't no broken glass,

Tons of trash
and uncut
grass over
there.

It boggles my mind all the time

How such a beautiful place

Could be filled with so much hate

Just like they said
they was going to
build a gate

To separate the
government
monkeys & the
apes.

Mmmmmmm...
didn't think about
that did you?

Although I did, like
the big green tower
standing tall and
proud

In a shower of
clouds, beautiful
wow.

If only it was like
that on the other
side.

It boggles my mind:

Separation, colonization

Colonization, separation

Say her name, say his name-

For our nation.

This, this very separation *is* the situation.

There are no complications.

Monkey can't you see?

Right now, as we speak a cop is probably choking one of us out while we yell, "I can't breathe." "Please help me, I can't breathe; stop, I can't breathe." But why should this be? I mean, we got puppets on the podium while the monkeys are silently killin' us on the streets.

I'm tired of askin'.

I demand to be free

No more all lives matter,

My life is the one that matters.

Black lives are the ones that matter.

This can't keep happening.

All this, I can't breathe - hands up, don't shoot, skittles and iced tea.

Separation,

Colonization,

                                        Separation,

Colonization.

It's all the same thing.

I liked that tall green.

Book made through the Illuminate: Literacy Entrepreneurs program of Know Allegiance Nation.

know allegiance nation

www.knowallegiance.org

Made in the USA
Columbia, SC
31 March 2024

33430008R10017